# A Town For All Seasons

Written By Eric J. Kregel

Illustrated By Olivia Wylie

This is a work of fiction. All of the characters, organizations, and events portrayed in this work are either products of the author's imagination or are used fictitiously.
A TOWN FOR ALL SEASONS
ISBN 978-1-7343271-4-4
Copyright © 2024 by Eric J. Kregel
Illustrated by Olivia Wylie
All rights reserved. No part of this publication may be reproduced, distributed, or transmitted in any form or by any means, including photocopying, recording, or other electronic or mechanical methods, without the prior written permission of the publisher, except in the case of brief quotations embodied in critical reviews and certain other noncommercial uses permitted by copyright law. For permission requests, write to the publisher at the address below.
Leafing Out Books
www.leafingoutgardening.com
Printed in the United States of America

Let's say a year is a town that can be walked within a day.

Who would you meet if you walked those streets?

What would you see?

Come with me, and I'll say...

Early in the frosty morning,
    you meet a January soul.

    Cold, aloof, and constant
January stands.

This grey figure stares you down.
You're a stranger, and something new as well.
New things don't suit January folk.

Cold, mercurial, and constant; that's the liturgy
embedded deep in these people, beneath the layers of
cotton down.

You can trust a January person, for routine shapes their lives.
   If it's morning, they tend to the heater,
if it's midday, they shovel.
If it's evening, they're closing up the home.

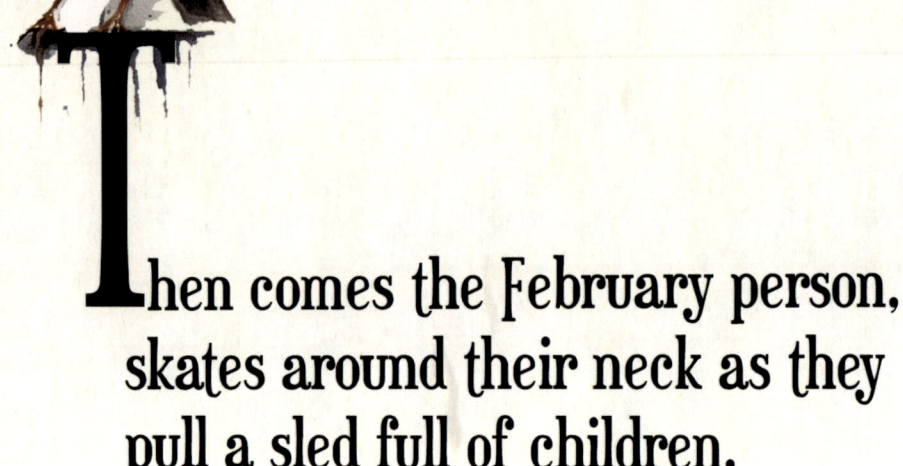

Then comes the February person, skates around their neck as they pull a sled full of children.

Defiant in the monochromatic face of winter, they seek no longer to settle and make do.

If the sidewalk is snowed over, they'll ski to work; if it's cold, they'll put extra marshmallows in their cocoa.

If their home is snowed in, they will go outside to remind their bodies that the sun still rises

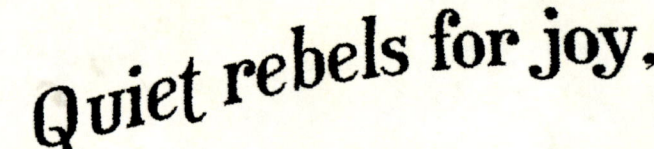

Quiet rebels for joy,

snow does not define the February folk.

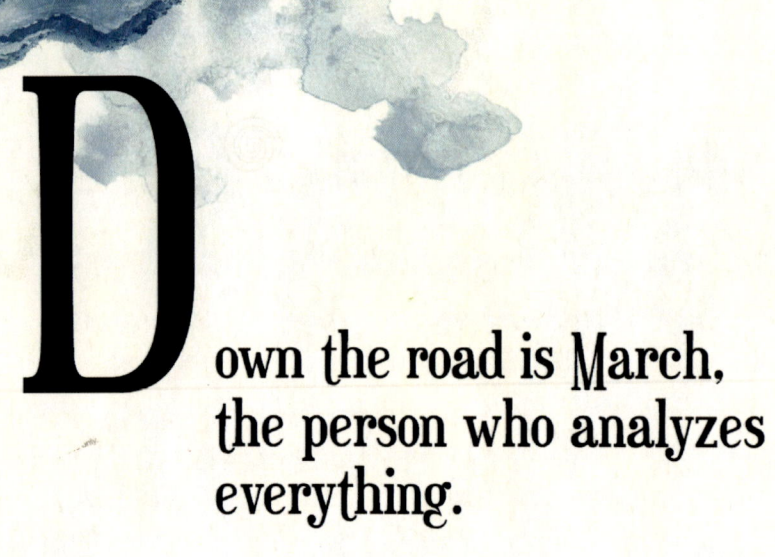

Down the road is March,
the person who analyzes
everything.

They watch the sky for birds, study the ground for moles, smell the air for pollen, and search for ladybugs in windowsills.

Studying,
　　　studying,
　　　　　studying:

　　　　　　　all for the sake
　　　　　　　　of making predictions.

How long will the snow last?

What will summer look like?

What to plant?

# Every question deserves an answer.

April walks alongside the March
 person on this day,
 laughing.

April people are the optimists of the neighborhood.

Winter cannot last, they say.
Everyone must wake up from a bad dream eventually.

The March person will doubt; the April person will smile.

"Sunshine must obey the law of statistics! Probability demands that the sun must shine any day now."

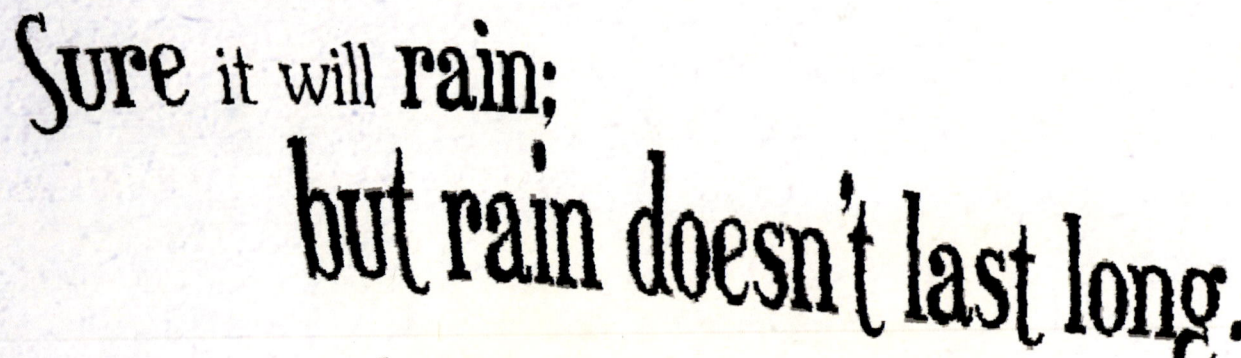

Sure it will rain; but rain doesn't last long.

You leave these two friends to bicker on the street and stroll by May, standing still as a statue near an empty park.

The May person is defined by many **forks** in their **roads**, divided by competing destinies.

Should they go **south** for the Summer? Or **north?**
Work on their home for the summer? Sell their home?
Educated by only **what could be,**
They are a **storehouse** of POTENTIAL
# RELISHING
in the **moment**
of
decision.

The afternoon warms your bones.

The sun rises high overhead,
presiding over the day.

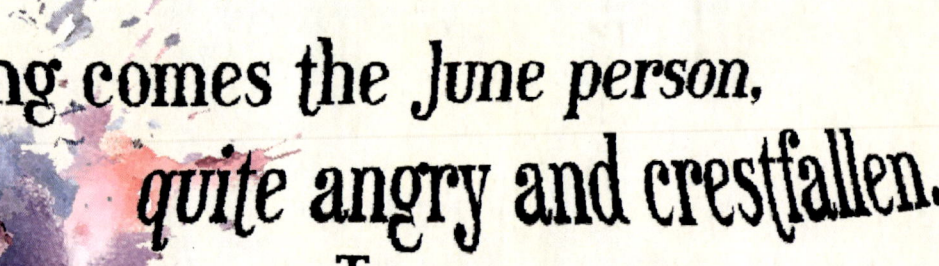

Along comes the June person, quite angry and crestfallen. Their happy sibling—

the May person—

isn't near them, because

June

is

driving

everyone

MAD.

Where the May person lives in **What Could Be**, June exists in the realm of **What Is Not**.

    Summer is here, they will moan. Then why is it raining, they will grumble.
    Summer is for planting, but who could plant in weather like this?

    June folk hear stories of February people and quickly dismiss those adventures; **anyone** can be heroic **in the cold.**

June is almost knocked flat by striding July.
July doesn't have time for June.

## THE SUN IS OUT.

How long it will shine,
no one can say.

These people are running to the lakesides,
calling the contractors to rebuild their homes,
　　　　　　working extra hours at the office,
setting up all the parties and reunions during summer break.

　They have no more room in the calendar for sleep, for sitting, for contemplation.
No, **they**
　　　　run
　　　　　　through
　　　　　　　　each
　　　　　　　　　　day.

ugust
        comes around the corner now,
          greeting you and frenetic July.
They smile and shuffle across the street
to an outdoor café.
            For this person of August,
              no one is a stranger.

Tanned with laugh lines and crows' feet around the eyes, they have embraced the season of long visits.

Get too close and you can smell charcoal from the BBQ, smoke from a fire pit, and gas from a quad.

They
    take
  long
walks
   around
    the
   neighborhood,
stopping
  and
    visiting.

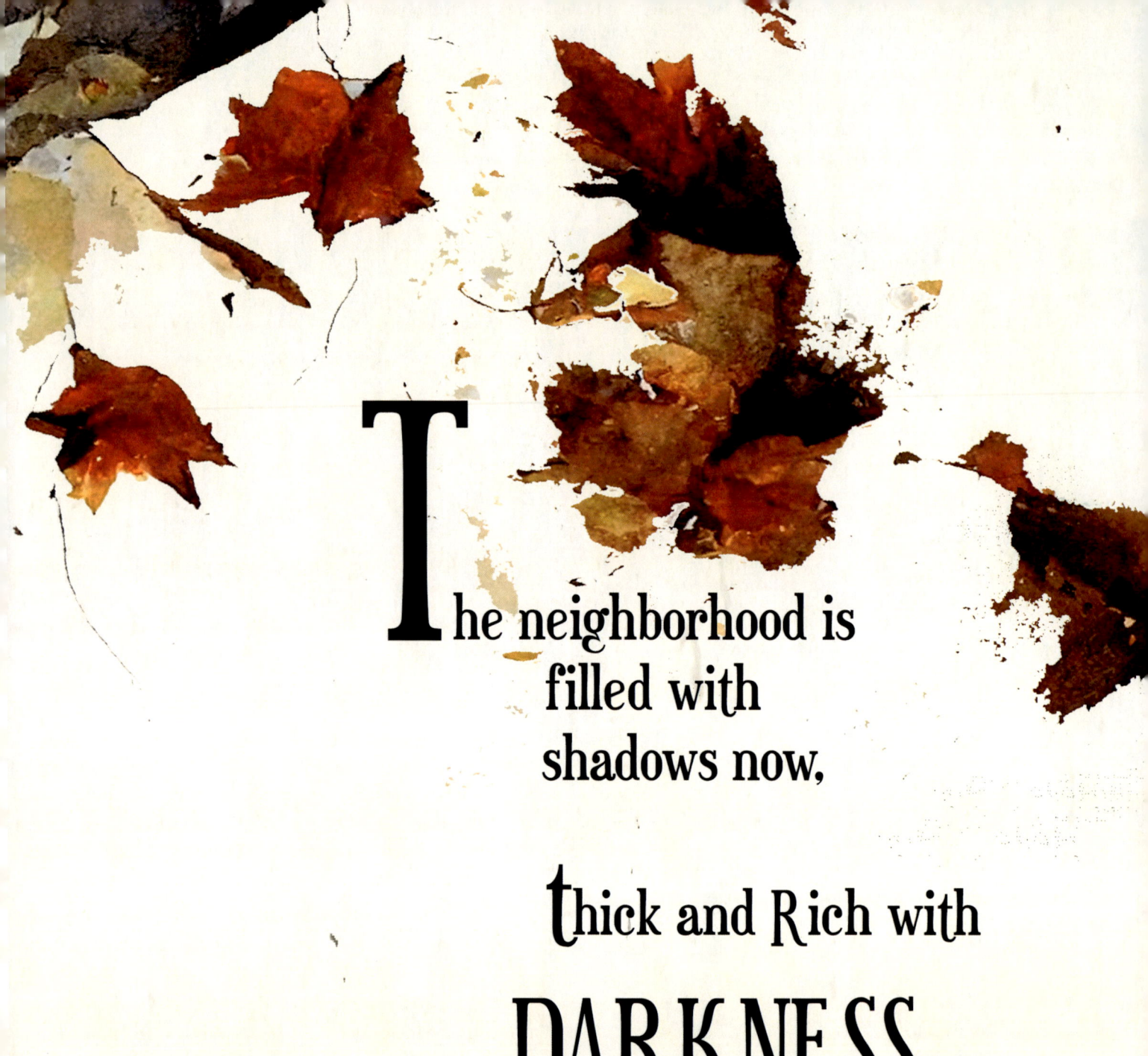

The neighborhood is filled with shadows now,

thick and Rich with

DARKNESS...

August's energy is shared by the September people. As you pass by the café, you can see them in the slim windows of their apartments.

THEIR HOBBIES ARE

* canning

* harvesting

* saving money and living off of lunches in brown bags.

Everything must be
saved,
stored,
and kept
clean.

'The snow is coming,
 the snow is coming...'

this is the mantra of September folk.

Responsibility is the heavy watch around their wrist, the ticking of their metabolism.

As you walk past the apartments, you come to a small park with a lone bench. This is where the October people sit and stare at the world.

They are watchful like the March people, but there is a bit more behind their eyes than analysis.

The leafless trees are no longer natural structures, but skeletons who dance with the wind.
Colors abound, telling autumnal tales.

The October people watch and listen and interpret, breathing in meaning.

# HALLOWEEN
## –the festival of walking metaphors –
### is their Christmas.

The snow is

coming...

You leave them and find the November person sitting on another bench, facing a barren field.

They sit within the suspended animation of those who bob in the sea of liminality.

November

is

waiting.

Waiting for the snow,

Waiting for the year to end,

Waiting for the new year to begin,

Waiting for the warmth to leave,

Waiting for a new season to begin,

Waiting,

Waiting,

Waiting...

**Y**ou walk on, and here at the town square you find the December person, radiant and glowing.

The year may be at an end, but now is the time of Christmas and Solstice and Change.

## December

speaks of hope wrapped up

and ready to be discovered,

joy hidden until the very end,

and the promise of a new kind of year

The December Person knows the end is in sight,

yet is neither worried nor angered by the passage.

December folk stand apart;

what they expect

no one else sees

or believes.

**No matter.**

# About The Author

Eric J. Kregel is a novelist, poet, Anglican Priest, and chaplain to the homeless in Edmonton, Canada. He has authored the rural Canadian steampunk novel "Exhaust from the Tin Woods" and has contributed several articles on faith, art, and magic. He is married with two daughters and a dog. You can find some of his writings: https://ericjkregel.wordpress.com/

# About The Artist

Olivia Wylie is a professional horticulturist and business owner who specializes in the restoration of neglected gardens. When the weather keeps her indoors, she enjoys researching and writing about the plant world and the complexities of being human. She lives in Colorado with a very patient husband and a rather impatient cat. Her works can be viewed at www.leafingoutgardening.com and https://www.oetearmann.com/

www.ingramcontent.com/pod-product-compliance
Lightning Source LLC
Chambersburg PA
CBRC091452160426
43209CB00023B/1878